John Foster

fireworords

A Book of Word Play Poems

designed and illustrated by
RIAN HUGHES

OXFORD
UNIVERSITY PRESS

On the Ning Nang Nong | Spike Milligan

On the Ning Nang Nong

Where the Cows go **BONG!**

And the Monkeys all say

There's a **Nong Nang Ning**

Where the trees go

And the tea pots **Jibber Jabber**

On the **Nong Ning Nang** All the mice go

So it's **Ning Nang Nong!**

Cows go **BONG!**

Nong Nang Ning!

Nong Ning Nang!
The mice go **CLANG**

What a noisy place to belong

Ping!

Joo.

ELANG!

And you just can't catch 'em when they do!

Trees go # Ping!

Is the **Ning Nang Ning Nang Nong!**

Barking Mad? | Tracey Blance

My Uncle Daniel
turned into a spaniel
so we gave him a **bone** for his tea.
We thought he'd be happier
but instead he grew snappier
and took a great chunk out of

me.

Uncle Ben from Number One | Brian Patten

Uncle Ben was not a hen
But when he laid an egg
He did it quite professionally
By lifting up a leg.

He studied it
and prodded it
And said,

'I'm mystified.'

And then he took it to the kitchen

where he ate it, fried.

Two Witches | Alexander Resnikoff

There was a witch
The witch had an itch
The itch was so itchy it
Gave her a twitch.

Another witch
Admired the twitch
So she started twitching
Though she had no itch.

Now both of them twitch
So it's hard to tell which
Witch has the itch and
Which witch has the twitch.

The Little Pig | Anon.

The lightning crashed, the thunder roared
Around the homestead station.
The little pig curled up his tail
And   ran   to   save   his   bacon.

Mississippi said to Missouri | Anon.

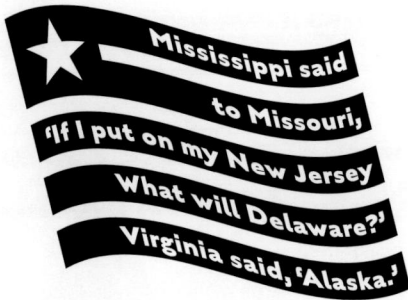

Mississippi said
to Missouri,
'If I put on my New Jersey
What will Delaware?'
Virginia said, 'Alaska.'

Burp | Anon.

Pardon me
for being so rude.
It was not me
it was my food.
It just came up
to say

HALLO!

Now it's gone
back down below.

The Ying-tong-iddle-I-po | Spike Milligan

My uncle Jim-jim
Had for years
Suffered from
Protruding ears.

Each morning then,
When he got up,
They stuck out like handles
On the FA Cup.

He tied them back
With bits of string
But they shot out again
With a noisy—PING!

They flapped in the wind
And in the rain,
Filled up with water
Then emptied again.

One morning Jim-jim
Fell out of bed
And got a Po
Stuck on his head.

He gave a Whoop,
A happy shout,
His ears no longer now
Stick out.

For the rest of his days
He wore that Po,
But now at night
He has nowhere to go.

Bedbugs Marching Song | John Agard

Bedbugs
Have the right
To bite.

Bedbugs
Of the world
Unite.

Don't let
These humans
Sleep too tight.

The Truth About the Abominable Footprint | Michael Baldwin

The Yeti's a Beast
Who lives in the East
  And suffers a lot from B.O.
His hot hairy feet
Stink out the street
  So he cools them off in the snow.

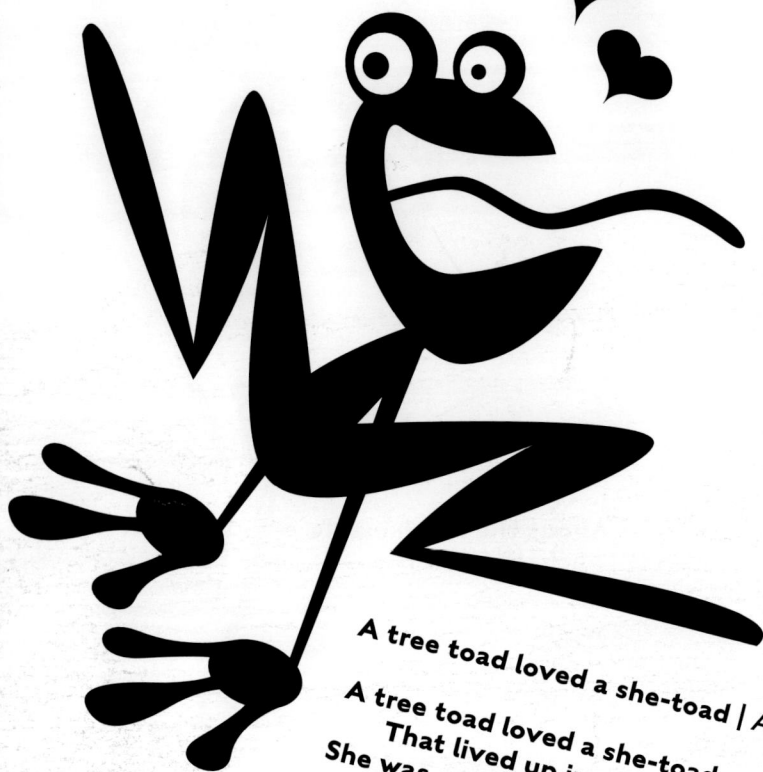

A tree toad loved a she-toad | Anon.

A tree toad loved a she-toad
That lived up in a tree.
She was a three-toed tree toad
But a two-toed toad was he.
The two-toed toad tried to win
The she-toad's friendly nod,
For the two-toed toad loved the ground
On which the three-toed toad trod.
But no matter how the two-toed tree toad tried,
He could not please her whim.
In her tree-toad bower,
With her three-toed power
The she-toad vetoed him.

Pop bottles pop-bottles
In pop shops;
The pop-bottles Pop bottles
Poor Pop drops.

When Pop drops pop-bottles
Pop-bottles plop!
Pop bottle-tops topple!
Pop mops slop!

Stop! Pop'll drop bottle!
Stop, Pop, stop!
When Pop bottles pop-bottles,
Pop-bottles pop!

Song of the Pop-Bottles
Morris Bishop

A canner exceedingly canny | Carolyn Wells

A canner exceedingly canny

One morning remarked to his granny

'A canner can can

Anything that he can

But a canner can't can a can, can he?'

Shaun Short's Short Shorts | John Foster

Shaun Short bought some shorts.
The shorts were shorter than Shaun Short thought.
Shaun Short's short shorts were so short,
Shaun Short thought, 'Shaun, you ought
Not to have bought shorts so short.'

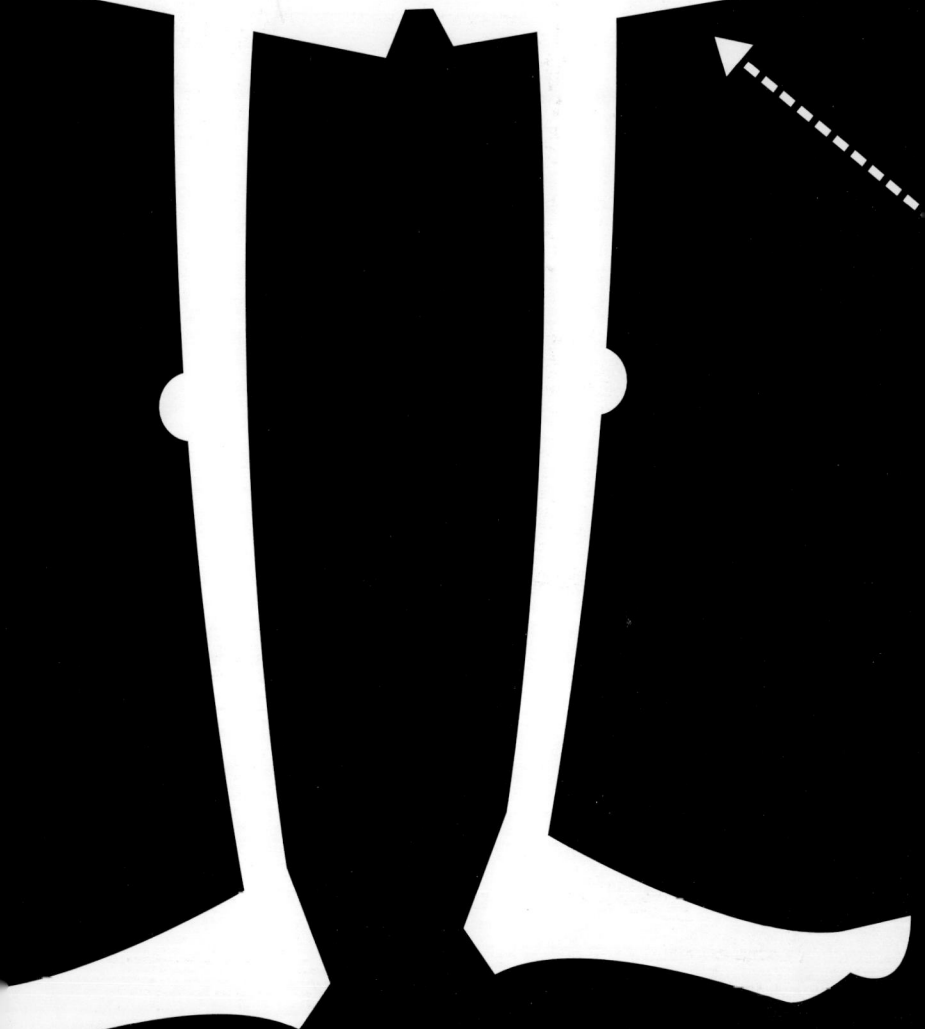

On mules we find two legs behind | Anon.

On mules we find two legs behind
And two we find before.
We stand behind before we find
What those behind be for.

We find before the two before
Just what they, too, be for.
So stand before the two behind
And behind the two before.

The Cow | Jack Prelutsky

The cow mainly **MOO**s as she chooses to **MOO**
   and she chooses to **MOO** as she chooses.

She furthermore chews as she chooses to chew
   and she chooses to chew as she muses.

If she chooses to **MOO** she may **MOO** to amuse
   or may **MOO** just to **MOO** as she chooses.

If she chooses to chew she may **MOO** as she chews
   or may chew just to chew as she muses.

To begin to toboggan, first buy a toboggan,
But don't buy too big a toboggan.
(A too big a toboggan is not a toboggan
To buy to begin to toboggan.)

Toboggan | Colin West

Say, did you say? | Anon.

Say, did you say, or did you not say
What I said you said?
For it is said that you said
That you did not say
What I said you said.
Now if you say that you did not say
What I said you said,
Then what do you say you did say
    instead
Of what I said you said?

?

A flea and a fly in a flue | Anon.

**A flea and a fly in a flue
Were imprisoned, so what could they do?**

Said the fly,

'Let us flee.'

Said the flea,

'Let us fly.'

So they flew through a flaw in the flue.

We saw Esau sitting on a see-saw,

who saw he saw, me or you?

See-Saw Rhyme | Colin Macfarlane

she saw we saw Esau too; he saw she saw we saw Esau . . .

I'm pig in the middle
Between two stools,
I sit on the fence
And obey the rules,
I face both ways,
I know the score.
That's what a pig
In the middle is for.

So-So Joe | John Agard

So-So Joe
de so-so man
wore a so-so suit
with a so-so shoe.
So-So Joe
de so-so man
lived in a so-so house
with a so-so view.
And when you asked
So-So Joe
de so-so man
How do you do?
So-So Joe
de so-so man
would say to you:
Just so-so
Nothing new.

Pig in the Middle | John Mole

I'm pig in the middle
I'm yes and no,
I'll come if you call
And I'm willing to go,
I fill the space,
Between either/or.
That's what a pig
In the middle is for.

Pig in the Middle | John Mole

Rant About Pants | Lindsay Macrae

Some people call them knickers
My granny calls them drawers
Hers used to keep the cold out
Now they're used for cleaning floors.

Florists call them bloomers
And lawyers call them briefs
While undertakers solemnly say
A pair of underneaths.

Fire fighters call them hosiery
Americans call them panties
Which are the nasty nylon kind
You get from distant aunties.

Small people call them long johns
Tall people call them shorts
There's even combinations
Designed to fit all sorts.

Lurking beneath a Scotsman's kilt
You're unlikely to find any
Which makes it nice and easy
When he wants to spend a penny.

There are bikinis, teeny-weenies
Trunks with no frills or fuss
You should always wear a fresh pair
In case you're knocked down by a bus.

There are hundreds of words for underwear
But I always call mine pants
They're white and clean and seldom seen
And they rhyme so well with ants.

The cheetah, my dearest,
is known not to cheat | George Barker

The cheetah, my dearest, is known not to cheat;
the tiger possesses no tie;
the horse-fly, of course, was never a horse;
the lion will not tell a lie.

The turkey, though perky, was never a Turk;
nor the monkey ever a monk;
the mandrel, though like one, was never a man,
but some men are like him, when drunk.

The springbok, dear thing, was not born in the spring;
the walrus will not build a wall.
No badger is bad; no adder can add.
There Is no truth in these things at all.

Wombat, Twobat | Sue Cowling

Wombat, twobat—
Didgeridoobat.
Threebat, fourbat—
Toreadorbat.
Fivebat, sixbat—
Bombaymixbat.
Sevenbat, eightbat—
EmpireStateBat.
Ninebat, tenbat—
You'reonagainbat!

Nicola Nicholas couldn't care less.
Nicola Nicholas tore her dress.
Nicola Nicholas tore her knickers.
Now Nicola Nicholas is knickerless.

Nicola Nicholas | John Foster

Hush-a-bye, gravy | Michael Rosen

Hush-a-bye, gravy, on the tree top;

When the wind blows the ladle will rock;

When the bough breaks the ladle will fall,

Down will come gravy, ladle and all.

Humpty Dumpty | Richard Edwards

Humpty Dumpty sat on a wall.
Humpty Dumpty had a great fall.
He didn't get bruised. He didn't get bumped,
Humpty Dumpty bungee-jumped.

Mary had a little lamb | Anon.

A lobster,

Mary had a little lamb,

and some prunes,

A glass of milk,

a piece of pie,

And then some macaroons.

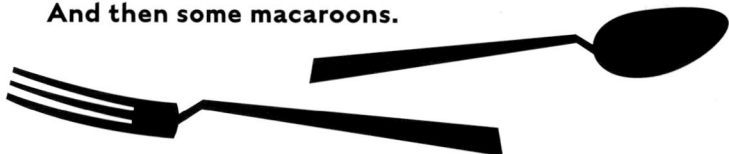

It made the busy waiters grin
To see her order so,
And when they carried Mary out,
Her face was white as snow.

Menu

Yankee Doodle | Bruce Lansky

Yankee Doodle went to town
riding on a chicken.
He went into a restaurant
and came out finger lickin'.

The Wolf's Rhyme | Catherine Storr

Monday's child is fairly tough,
Tuesday's child is tender enough,
Wednesday's child is good to fry,
Thursday's child is best in pie,
Friday's child makes good meat roll,
Saturday's child is casserole,
But the child that is born on the Sabbath day
Is delicious when eaten in any way.

Pussycat, Pussycat | Max Fatchen

Pussycat, pussycat, where have you been,
Licking your lips with your whiskers so clean?
Pussycat, pussycat, purring and pudgy,
Pussycat, pussycat, WHERE IS OUR BUDGIE?

Old Mother Hubbard | Anon.

Old Mother Hubbard
Went to the cupboard
To get her poor dog a bone.
When she got there,
The cupboard was bare,
And she said

OICURMT!

I had a little nut tree | Richard Edwards

I had a little nut tree
The tree said, 'Oi!
I gave the tree a whack,
You naughty boy!'
And whacked me sharply back.

Hush-a-bye, Baby | Anon.

Hush-a-bye, baby,
Your milk's in the tin.
Mummy has got you
A nice sitter-in.

Hush-a-bye, baby,
Now don't give a frown,
While Mummy and Daddy
Go out on the town.

Little Bo-Peep | Michael Dugan

Little Bo-Peep has lost her sheep,
gee, that girl is dumb.
She'd lose her teeth if they weren't
stuck into her gum.

Egg | Coral Rumble

I am an egg living in a world where egg beating is allowed, even encouraged, and so I am whipped round and round, until I am dizzy with the pain and longing for those shy days before I came out of my shell.

Poem with a Hole | Noel Petty

A doughnut
I would never groan at.
However many I've had before
I can always eat just one more.
Our maths teacher used to bore us
by telling us its shape was a torus.
but there's a far more curious riddle
About the hole in the middle
Do you suppose that they make
A long doughy sort of snake
Then chop off the short strings
And glue them up into rings?
Or make a blob and then bore
A circular hole through the core?
And if the latter, how do they decide
Who gets to eat the bit from inside?
And here's a question to examine:
How do they get the jam in?
A problem you can attack
After a snack

I am
the crazy
crater creature,
I creep across the
crater 's cracks
and cr u nch the
crimson crystals
that cringe in
crooked cul-de-sacs.
Once a crumbling spacecraft crashed—
an ancient cosmonaut crawled clear.
Across the crinkled crust I chased her
and chortling with churlish cheer
caught the granny
in a cranny
of the crater
and ate her

creature | Dave Calder

the
thing
that
I
like
about
string
is
the
way
that it loops and it twists and it
makes knots that are really difficult to undo.

Blackhead of a greasy skin

Hallowe'en Hot-Pot | Gina Douthwaite

in the cauldron simmering,
hair of nose and wax of ear,
scurf of scalp and salt of tear,
sticky eye and fur of tongue,
plaque of tooth and blood of gum.
For a spell stir at the double,
bring it to the boil
and bubble.

Watch | Gina Douthwaite

1 is a left-handed arrow.

2 is kneeling in prayer.

3's a bare bottom bent over.

4 is a nose with one hair.

5 is the stroke of a swimmer.

6 —sellotape at an end.

7's a 'Z' that's not quite asleep

8 —specs on a cock-eyed friend.

9's the last sheet on the roll.

10 is a slot and a coin.

11's a gate held wide open

12 —a swan swims to a groyne.

Vlad ve
vampire vlies
vrough voonlight
velvet vat vings vlitter-
vlutter. Vlad's very vain vith
vangs vo vlong vey vite
vrough vlesh vlike vutter.
Vlad vears a vast vile
violet vest villed vith
vermin vrom ve vault
vich vongs vorse van
virty vultures—vo
vonder victims
vaint vand
vall! Vicious,
vulgar, vlood-
vrinking, vad,
violent,
villainous—
vot a vlad

Vlad | Dave Calder

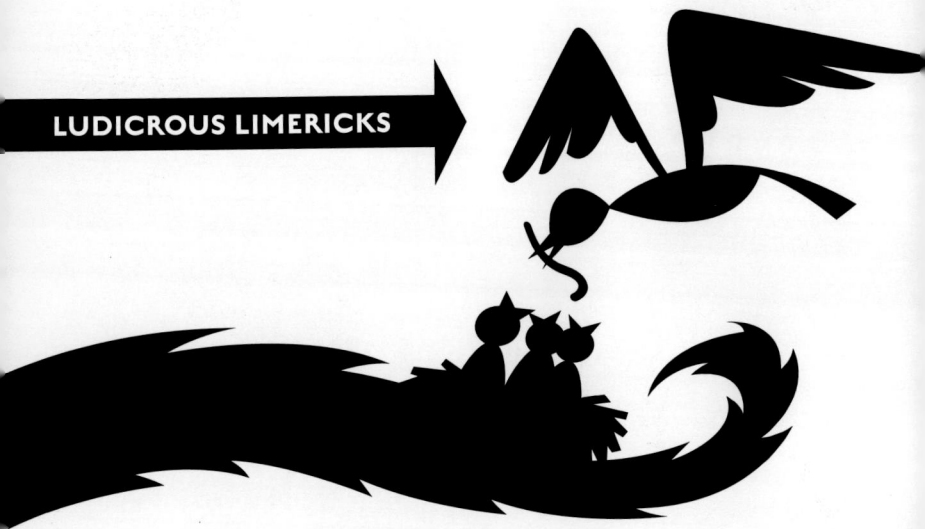

The Bearded Old Man | Edward Lear

There was an old man with a beard,
Who said, 'It is just as I feared!—
    Two Owls and a Hen,
    Four Larks and a Wren,
Have all built their nests in my beard!'

A curious fellow named Kurt | Michael Palin

A curious fellow named Kurt
Used to climb Alpine peaks in a skirt.
He said it felt nice
In the snow and the ice;
And it kept those below more alert.

There was a young lady of Riga | Anon.

There was a young lady of Riga,
Who went for a ride on a tiger:
  They returned from the ride
  With the lady inside
And a smile on the face of the tiger.

1 2 3

Howard | A. A. Milne

There was a young puppy called Howard,
Who at fighting was rather a coward,
   He never quite ran
   When the battle began
But he started at once to bow-wow hard.

The Old Fellow of Tyre | Anon.

There was an old fellow of Tyre,
Who constantly sat on the fire.
　　When asked, 'Are you hot?'
　　He said,

'Certainly not.
I'm James Winterbotham, Esquire.'

There was an old lady from Ryde | Anon.

There was an old lady from Ryde
Who ate some bad apples and died.
   The apples fermented
   Inside the lamented
And made cider inside her inside.

70° proof

There was a young parson named Perkins | Anon.

There was a young parson named Perkins
Exceedingly fond of small gherkins.
   One summer at tea
   He ate forty-three,
Which pickled his internal workings.

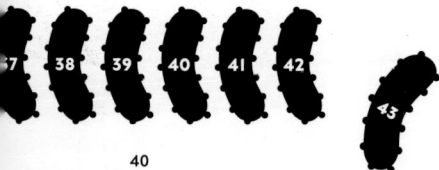

37   38   39   40   41   42   43

An explorer named Mortimer Craft | Mick Gowar

An explorer named Mortimer Craft,
While in Africa ate spiced giraffe.
   The effect of this food
   Was a sound deep and rude
And green flames that shot out fore and aft.

OCCUPIED

There was a faith-healer of Deal | Lewis Carroll

There was a faith-healer of Deal
Who said, 'Although pain isn't real
   If I sit on a pin
   And I puncture my skin,
I dislike what I fancy I feel.'

OUCH!

A cheerful old Bear at the Zoo | Lewis Carroll

A cheerful old bear at the Zoo
Could always find something to do.
   When it bored him to go
   On a walk to and fro
He reversed it, and walked fro and to.

Nelly Ninnis | Spike Milligan

There was a young girl called Nelly
Who had a nylon belly
The skin was so thin
We could all see in
It was full of custard and jelly.

A greedy young scrumper called Sue | Marian Swinger

A greedy young scrumper called Sue
scoffed apples, pears, greengages too.
She consumed every core,
then scrumped a few more
and spent all the next day on the loo.

Said a porcupine:
'Dear Miss Pin Cushine,
It's for you I pine;
I wish you were mine . . .

Will you be my Valentine?'

Courtship | Alexander Resnikoff

Said Miss Pin Cushion:
'My dear Porcupin,
It's really a sin
But me you cannot win—

IF YOU DON'T KNOW THE DIFFERENC[E]
Between PINE and PIN!'

Banananananananananana | William Cole

I thought I'd win the spelling bee
   And get right to the top,
But I started to spell banana,
   And I didn't know when to stop.

A pretty deer | Anon.

A pretty deer is dear to me,
   A hare with downy hair;
A hart I love with all my heart,
   But barely bear a bear.

'Tis plain that no one takes a plane
   To get a pair of pears,
Although a rake may take a rake
   To tear away the tares.

Beer often brings a bier to man,
   Coughing a coffin brings,
And too much ale will make us ail,
   As well as other things.

Quails do not quail before a storm,
   A bough will bow before it;
No human hand can rein the rain—
   No earthly power reigns o'er it.

The new gnus | John Foster

A gnu who was new to the zoo
Asked another gnu what he should do.

The other gnu said, shaking his head,
'If I knew, I'd tell you, I'm new too!'

Whoosh! Cheetah! | Wes Magee

A member of the Cat family
and sucH a speedy sprintah.
It racEs across Africa's plains
to catch antelopE and zebrah.
Can climb a Tree with agilitee,
and is All quicksilver speed. A dashah.
Whoosh! CheetaH!

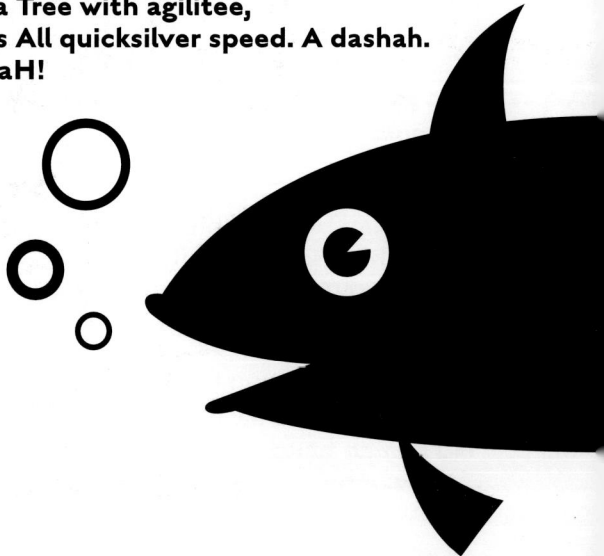

If the plural of house is houses
and the plural of mouse is mice
why then the plural of rouses
should surely be written as rice

and if the plural of deer is deer
and the plural of fish is fish
then the plural of beer should be beer
and the plural of dish should be dish

If mouses run over our houses
and eat up our loaves and our scones
why then our lice should be louses
and our phones should be sounded as phons.

Spelling Game | Iain Crichton Smith

An Unspelling Bea | John Cotton

An unspelling bea, an unspelling bea
i buzz abart for ours u sea
Amungst blewbells and croakuses
And other flours, not making a fuss
As i serch for hunny and land on pedals
Making sure that nobody medals
With this sharp-stinging
Humming-singing
Unspelling bea
Who seams to have lost his dictionree.

Spelling Bee | David McCord

It takes a good speller
to spell cellar,
separate, and benefiting;
not omitting
cemetery, cataclysm,
picnicker and pessimism.
And have you ever tried
innocuous, inoculate,
desert, deserted, desiccate;
divide and spied,
gnat, knickers, gnome,
crumb, crypt and chrome;
surreptitious, supersede,
delete, dilate, impede?

Here lies
The body
Of Annabel Smedley
Who took an eternity pill
Which proved deadly

Here lies
The top half
Of 'Dithering' Freddy
The rest will come soon
When it feels
That it's ready

RIPs (Really Implausible People) | Lindsay Macrae

Epitaph for John Bun | Anon.

Here lies John Bun.
He was killed by a gun.
His name was not Bun, but Wood,
But Wood would not rhyme with
gun, but Bun would.

Here lie
The ashes
Of Jim 'Houseproud'
Groover
Who sucked himself up
With a powerful Hoover

Here lie
The remains
Of 'Fast' Eddy Jakes
Who invented a sports car
Without any brakes

Epitaph for Number Nine | Ian Whybrow

Our centre forward's passing
Has been United's loss.
His final words were 'On me head'
So there we placed this cross.

9

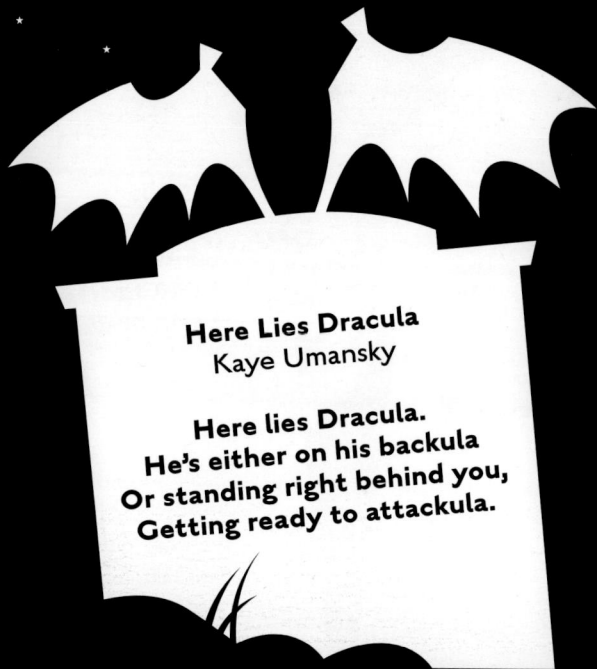

Here Lies Dracula
Kaye Umansky

Here lies Dracula.
He's either on his backula
Or standing right behind you,
Getting ready to attackula.

Epitaph for Frankenstein | Clive Webster

When Frankenstein's Monster finally died,
And his reign of terror ceased,
These were the words they inscribed on his grave:

May the occupant
Rust in Peace

Epitaph for a Golfer | Anon.

1

This golfer here
would swing
his clubs
till time
at last took toll.
Now in this grave
below this stone,
he's reached
his final hole.

Hiya, Cynth. | Wes Magee

'Please mark my grave
with just one flower.'
That was the wish
of Cynthia Tower.
So when she died
they raised a plinth
and marked upon it

Hiya, Cynth.

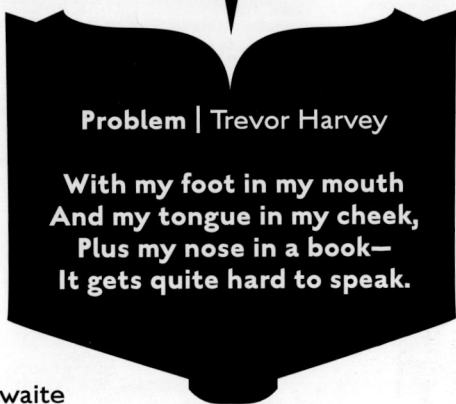

Problem | Trevor Harvey

With my foot in my mouth
And my tongue in my cheek,
Plus my nose in a book—
It gets quite hard to speak.

Cross Words | Gina Douthwaite

```
                    t
      t         w h a m
      r i p         r         d
      i           a   t w i s t           s   s   s c r a p
      p o k e     s   h   g u           s l a n g   h
        i         s h o u t     g r i p       a   a   u
      b   c l a w     m     c         u   s p i t   c
w r e c k     e     p u l l         n   n     c h o k e
h a     s h a k e         o   s   c       a       h
a   t     n   r         h u r l   h u r t
c     s   e     s t a b     t     i         l
k   w r e n c h     i       n   j
      a     r     o   f   s   g r a b
      t     r a v e   f l o g   b a n g
      b     a   e         c       t
      a     n     k n o c k     h i t
      s c r a t c h       u         l e t ' s
      h                   f         b e
                          f         e s
                                    s
                          m a t e s
```

Tantrums | Roger McGough

When my sister starts to frown
I'm always on my guard

Yesterday she threw a tantrum
But it missed me by a yard.

Naming the Days | Dave Calder

Sun's day, Moon's day, Tiw's day, Woden's day,
Thor's day, Frig's day, Saturn's day

Someday, Mum's day, Choose day, Wooden day,
Thought day, Fry day, Slacker day

Such fun day, Monster bun day, To snooze day, Wet nose sneeze day,
Furry purrs day, Fly away day, Sit and natter day

Short run day, Maths begun day, True news day, Red knees day,
Thirsty day, Fish-pie day, Scatter day

Every day's different, never repeated, unique:
What names would you give the days this week?

Cried Frankenstein's Monster:

By heck!
I feel like a physical wreck!
My face has more stitches
Than two pairs of britches
And these bolts are a pain in the neck!

Angry Loo Haiku | Lindsay Macrae

People think it's fun
to pull my handle and quip:
'You look a bit flushed!'

Quasimodo | Willis Hall

'The Hunchback?' said Esmeralda.
'Yes. I know the man quite well.
His name is hard to remember,
But his face sure rings a bell!'

Space Joke | Julie Holder

'Knock, knock,' said the Astronaut.
'Who's there?' said the Alien.
'A Human Being,' said the Astronaut.
'A Human being what?' said the Alien.

The Loofah | Colin West

The loofah feels he can't relax,
For something is amiss:
He scratches other people's backs,
But no one scratches his.

I sleep upon
a bed of nails.
I must confess
it never fails
To help me get
a good night's rest,
And, overall,
I'm most impressed.

Bed of Nails | Colin West

Animal Chatter | Gyles Brandreth
a piece of doggerel

The other morning, feeling dog-tired,
    I was walking sluggishly to school,
When I happened upon two girls I know—
    who were busy playing the fool.
They were monkeying about, having a fight—
But all that they said didn't sound quite right.
'You're batty, you are—and you're catty too.'
'That's better than being ratty, you peevish shrew!'
'Don't be so waspish!' 'Don't be such a pig!'
'Look who's getting cocky—your head's too big!'
'You silly goose! Let me have my say!'
'Why should I, you elephantine popinjay?!'
I stopped, I looked, I listened—and I had to laugh
Because I realized then, of course,
    it's never the cow or the calf
That behave in this bovine way.
It's mulish humans like those girls I met the other day.
You may think I'm too dogged,
    but something fishy's going on—
The way we beastly people speak of animals
    is definitely wrong.
Crabs are rarely crabby and mice are never mousy
(And I believe all lice deny that they are lousy).
You know, if I wasn't so sheepish and if I had my way
I'd report the English language to the RSPCA.

Lime Lodge,
Lemon Lane,
Leek.

Chewsday

Dear Cress and Carrot,

Juice to let you know
that Melon I
are giving a parsnip.

Please bring pumpkin to drink.

Papaya for now,

Logan Berry

Herb House,
Rhubarb Road,
Broccoli.

Thirstday

Dear Logan,

Thanks for your pepper
dated last Chewsday.
Asparagus know
we'll turnip.

Yours tastefully,

Cress and Carrot

Alphabet Grumble | Julie Holder

A1 means the very best
B4 all the rest and B side
C side is my
D light where
E gulls soar 2
Farenheits but now,
G whizz, the
H2O has turned to
Ice and summer's
Joyz
K.o.
Lectric light instead of sun and beaches
MT of
NE1.
O shun roars and cold waves toss and
P pull
Q4 bread not candyfloss.
R√ ice and R√ snow make me feel like an
S kimo but
T times toasting bread and toes
U sually cure some winter woes like
V iews of wintry weather maps and
W s of socks and hats,
X press a wish for spring's return
Y not but for now I've
Z it's winter's turn and so this alphabet.(full stop)

Short Words | Colin West

Short words that we use, such as **bee, bat,** or **bird,**
Go under a name quite inapt and absurd:
No wonder this adjective seldom is heard,
For **monosyllabic,** I fear is the word.

Didgeridoo | Roger McGough

Catfish
take catnaps on seabeds
Sticklebacks
stick like glue
Terrapins
are teriffic with needles
But what does a didgery do?

Bloodhounds
play good rounds of poker
Chihuahuas
do nothing but chew
Poodles
make puddles to paddle in
But what does a didgery do?

A puffin
will stuff in a muffin
A canary
can nearly canoe
Humming-birds
hum something rotten
But what does a didgery do?

Tapeworms
play tapes while out jogging
Flies
feed for free at the zoo
Headlice
use headlights at night-time
But what does a didgery do?

What does a didgery
What does a didgery
What does a didgery do?

Neck which stretches high,
Patchwork skin in brown and gold,
A strange sight running.

Arachnid by name,
Enemy to careless flies,
Known to persevere.

WRIGGLING RIDDLES

Guess Who Haiku
Daphne Kitching

1

2

my mum is your mum
my big sister
always goes around
with your big sister
when I kiss you
you kiss me
but when
I raise my right fist
to try and hit you
you catch it with your left
I can see you
but I'm never quite sure
if you can see me
I know
who I am
but
who knows
who you are
?

my mum is your mum | Dave Ward

my mum is your mum
my big sister
always goes around
with your big sister
when I kiss you
you kiss me
but when
I raise my right fist
to try and hit you
you catch it with your left
I can see you
but I'm never quite sure
if you can see me
I know
who I am
but
who knows
who you are
?

Small furry mammal,
Long, radar ears, twitching nose,
Often called Peter.

Uninvited guests,
Small, scurrying night raiders,
Addicted to cheese.

3

4

Guess
Berlie Doherty

My first is in rattle but not in creak
my second's in creak but not in squeak
my third is in squeak and also in squeal
my fourth is in whistle and also in shrill
my fifth is in clanking and clanging and iron
my whole is a monster who roars on the line.

A Riddle | Jonathan Swift

Because I am by nature blind,
I wisely choose to walk behind;
However, to avoid disgrace,
I let no creature see my face.
My words are few, but spoke with sense:
And yet my speaking gives offence:
Or, if to whisper I presume,
The company will fly the room.
By all the world I am oppressed,
But my oppression gives them rest.

A Riddle | Christina Rossetti

There is one that has a head without an eye,
    And there's one that has an eye without a head.
You may find the answer if you try;
    And when all is said,
Half the answer hangs upon a thread.

What am I? To follow closely where you go to stretch in places where you grow, to hold together blood and bones, to fit round compl icated zones, to be a bree ding ground for spots, to pim ple, sweat, and smell because to be around you is my lot—to stick with you until we rot.

My Job Is: | Gina Douthwaite

Some   are
tied but others wag—
get a taste for telling tales,
thum are thyort, at length
some nag, stuck out ones
r e v e a l   w h a t   a i l s
or are seen, when others
hold theirs, as a show
of outright cheek.
I n - c h e e k   o n e s
will try to tease,
no matter what
tongue, so
to speak

Clues to Chew Over
Gina Douthwaite

What am I?

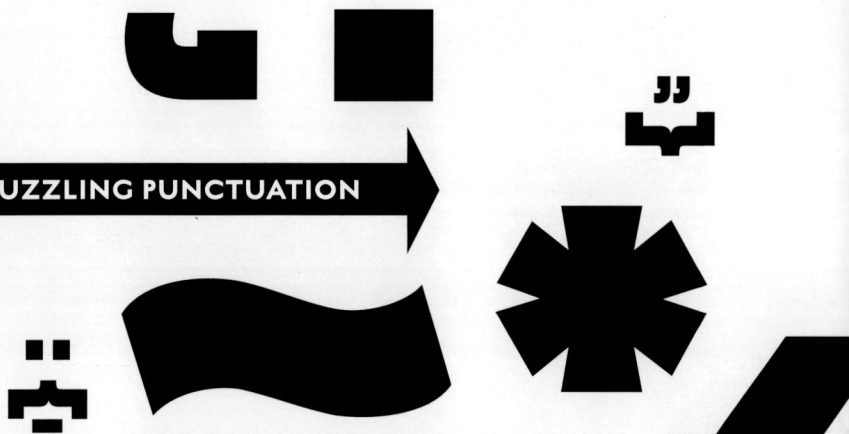

Caesar entered on his head | Anon.

Caesar entered on his head
A helmet on each foot
A sandal in his hand he had
His trusty sword to boot

Every lady in the land | Anon.

Every lady in the land
    Has twenty nails on each hand
Five and twenty on hands and feet
    This is true without deceit.

A Family Meal | Wendy Cope

'Put it on,' the table said.
Mother, when I brought the bread,
Tasted good. Dad licked. His lips,
Both of them, liked fish. And chips
Wash up. 'Please do it now,' asked Mother,
Looking at me. 'And rob my brother.'
Dad stretched the budgie, chattered on,
'How sad to think.' Those days are gone.

PREPOSTEROUS PUNS

Raising Frogs for Profit | Anon.

**Raising frogs for profit
Is a very sorry joke.
How can you make money
When so many of them croak?**

Newton heard a sort of plonk | Cyril Fletcher

Newton heard a sort of plonk— An apple fell upon his conk;

Discovered gravitation law, It shook old Isaac to the core.

Punishment | Eric Finney

An orange instead of an egg—
That's what the brown hen made!
And the chick's astonished comment was:
'Look what marmalade!'

We've got this sauce competition
Going in our family:
I'm half-way down the salad cream,
Dad's nearly finished his H.P.
Mum, though, has only just started
Her favourite sauce:
It's up tomato ketchup, of course.

Got this smashing new
Continental quilt
In stripes of pink and grey,
And now sheets, blankets,
Eiderdowns
Don't seem necessary
Duvet?

You may think I'm
Joking
When I tell you
I'm buying
Lord of the Rings
With my
Book Tolkien.

The Terns | Spike Milligan

Said the mother Tern
   to her baby Tern

Would you like a brother?

      Said Baby Tern
         to Mother Tern

Yes
One good Tern deserves another.

71

INDEX OF TITLES AND FIRST LINES

First lines are in light type

ANSWERS TO RIDDLES

ACKNOWLEDGEMENTS

We are grateful to the authors for permission to include the following poems, all of which are published for the first time in this collection

Petonelle Archer: 'String Song', copyright © Petonelle Archer 2000; Tracey Blance: 'Barking Mad?', copyright © Tracey Blance 2000; Dave Calder: 'Naming the Days', copyright © Dave Calder 2000; Wendy Cope: 'A Family Meal', copyright © Wendy Cope 2000; John Cotton: 'An Unspelling Bea', copyright © John Cotton 2000; Sue Cowling: 'Wombat, Twobat', copyright © Sue Cowling 2000; Michael Dugan: 'Little Bo-Peep', copyright © Michael Dugan 2000; John Foster: 'Nicola Nicholas', copyright © John Foster 2000; Mick Gower: 'An Explorer Named Mortimer Craft', copyright © Mick Gower 2000; Trevor Harvey: 'Problem', copyright © Trevor Harvey 2000; Julie Holder: 'Alphabet Grumble', copyright © Julie Holder 2000; Colin Macfarlane: 'See-Saw Rhyme', copyright © Colin Macfarlane 2000; Wes Magee: 'Whoosh! Cheetah' and 'Hiya, Cynth', both copyright © Wes Magee 2000; John Mole: 'Pig in the Middle', copyright © John Mole 2000; Noel Petty: 'Poem with a Hole', copyright © Noel Petty 2000; Coral Rumble: 'Egg', copyright © Coral Rumble 2000; Iain Crichton Smith: 'Spelling Game', copyright © Iain Crichton Smith 2000; Marian Swinger: 'A Greedy Young Scrumper Named Sue', copyright © Marian Swinger 2000; Clive Webster: 'Epitaph for Frankenstein', copyright © Clive Webster 2000

We also acknowledge permission to include previously published poems: John Agard: 'Bed Bugs Marching Song' from We Animals Would Like a Word With you (Bodley Head Children's Books), reprinted by permission of Random House UK Ltd; 'So-So Joe' from No Hickory, No Dickory, No Dock (Puffin Books, 1991), reprinted by permission of John Agard, c/o Caroline Sheldon Literary Agency; Michael Baldwin: 'The Truth About the Abominable Footprint' from Monster Poems compiled by John Foster (OUP), reprinted by permission of the author; George Barker: 'The cheetah, my dearest, is known not to cheat' from Runes and Rhymes and Tunes and Chimes (Faber & Faber Ltd), reprinted by permission of the publisher; Morris Bishop: 'Song of the Pop-Bottles', originally published in The New Yorker, © The New Yorker 1950, reprinted by permission of Condé Nast Publications. All rights reserved; Gyles Brandreth: 'Animal Chatter' first published in A Fourth Poetry Book compiled by John Foster (OUP), reprinted by permission of the author; Dave Calder: 'Creature', copyright © Dave Calder 1998, first published in Word Whirls (OUP 1998); 'Vlad', copyright © Dave Calder 1997, first published in Tongue Twisters and Tonsil Twizzlers (Macmillan, 1997), both reprinted by permission of the author; Berlie Doherty: 'Guess' from Walking on Air (HarperCollins), reprinted by permission of David Higham Associates Ltd; Gina Douthwaite: 'Clues to Chew Over', copyright © Gina Douthwaite 1998; 'Hallowe'en Hot-Pot', copyright © Gina Douthwaite 1998, first published in Word Whirls edited by John Foster, (OUP, 1998); 'My Job Is', copyright © Gina Douthwaite 1996, first published in Nothing Tastes Quite Like a Gerbil edited by David Orme, (Macmillan Children's Books, 1996), 'Watch', 'Crosswords', and 'Chew Lettuce', copyright © Gina Douthwaite

OXFORD
UNIVERSITY PRESS

Great Clarendon Street Oxford OX2 6DP

Oxford | New York
Athens | Auckland | Bangkok | Bogotá | Buenos Aires | Calcutta | Cape Town |
Chennai | Dar es Salaam | Delhi | Florence | Hong Kong | Istanbul | Karachi |
Kuala Lumpur | Madrid | Melbourne | Mexico City | Mumbai | Nairobi | Paris |
São Paulo | Singapore | Taipei | Tokyo | Toronto | Warsaw
and associated companies in: Berlin | Ibadan

Oxford is a trade mark of Oxford University Press

Designed and illustrated by Rian Hughes at Device: www.devicefonts.co.uk.

First published 2000

British Library Cataloguing in Publication Data available

ISBN 0 19 276243 5 (hardback)
ISBN 0 19 276244 3 (paperback)

Printed in Hong Kong